Psalm 119:

—— *The Supremacy of God's Word* ——

Ron Hirschhorn

WestBow
P R E S S
A DIVISION OF THOMAS NELSON

WestBow Press books may be ordered through booksellers or by contacting:

WestBow Press
A Division of Thomas Nelson
1663 Liberty Drive
Bloomington, IN 47403
www.westbowpress.com
1-(866) 928-1240

ISBN: 978-1-4497-3153-3 (sc)
ISBN: 978-1-4497-3152-6 (e)

Library of Congress Control Number: 2011960656

Printed in the United States of America

WestBow Press rev. date: 12/05/2011

To my wife, Lisa, and daughters, Deborah & Rebekah, with all my love.

Also, in loving memory of Debra Ann Wieber, June 3, 1964 - June 6, 1981

Acknowledgements:

Mr. Gene Podrazik for his skillful editing of the manuscript.

Dr. Jim and Carol Ausfahl for their proofreading and prayers. Your friendship and encouragement are always appreciated!

Preface: My Story

When you purchase books or music written by a "Christian" have you ever stopped to think that you are "buying" into their Christian walk? Are you familiar with his or her story of how and why the author or composer accepted Jesus as Savior and Lord? The substance of that person's work usually shows the depth of their commitment. By way of keeping it real, this is my story.

I was born and raised on Long Island, New York, as the youngest of three sons in a Jewish family. I use the term "Jewish" loosely since we didn't practice our religion nor partake in any Jewish traditions. For all intents and purposes I was just like most boys my age. I played ball in the neighborhood, watched sports and cartoons on television, went to school and played in the school band.

At the beginning of my high school senior year in September 1980 I had a conversation with Patti, one of my classmates. I had known Patti since sixth grade, through band

and common classes. We talked about how we spent our summer. I talked about mine, and then she said something quite peculiar about the big event in her summer.

"I got healed and I got saved."

I replied, "You got what and what?"

She proceeded to share with me the details of how and why she accepted Jesus as her Savior and Lord. I listened, thought it was interesting, but certainly not for me.

During the course of our senior year Patti periodically shared the Gospel with me. By the latter part of the school year I told her, "I don't know what I'm supposed to be about, as a Jew. Don't tell me how to be a Christian." And that stopped the conversation.

On June 3, 1981 a member of the band named Debbie Wieber was involved in a serious car accident. Debbie was a junior, a member of the Honor Society, and the cutest clarinet player in the band. I had a silent crush on her from afar. The car accident, which happened on her seventeenth birthday, left her brain damaged and breathing only on a respirator. She died on June 6, 1981.

I was completely devastated. How could God take someone who had her whole life ahead of her, could've excelled in any vocation she chose, but leave someone like me behind, who would only become one of the many cogs in the business machine? I didn't understand all this.

Shortly thereafter I did two things: 1) I bought a Bible intending to learn about my Jewish heritage, and 2) I began attending synagogue to see the Jewish faith put into practice.

I started reading Genesis and continued to read a chapter almost every night. My goal was to understand the context of what was written. This provided a solid basis for a correct interpretation of that day's reading.

I attended a couple of Reform synagogues where the least amount of Hebrew was spoken as part of the service. My desire was to see how Judaism was put into action on an everyday basis.

During the next four years I learned two things. 1) Reading the Hebrew Scriptures (commonly known as the Old Testament) gave me an appreciation of my Jewish heritage. 2) Attending synagogue was partaking in a religious tradition. It seemed that the two were divergent paths at odds with one another. By age 21 I stopped attending synagogue but continued with my Bible reading.

Also during this time I had been challenged to think about the claims that Jesus was the Jewish Messiah. As a Jew I naturally dismissed it. Judaism was on one side of the fence, Christianity the other. And the two were never intended to come together, right?

By age 22 I decided to resolve the issue. I determined to read the New Testament but discount everything that Jesus had to say about Himself. I wanted to read where God affirmed Jesus as Messiah. It didn't take long. Very early in Matthew's Gospel it read, "And lo a voice from heaven, saying, This is my beloved Son, in whom I am well pleased" (KJV). Jesus did not make the Messiah claim about Himself. God affirmed it.

It took two years to complete reading the New Testament at the rate of a chapter almost every night. Altogether it took me six years to read the Bible cover-to-cover just once.

At the age of twenty four I met a co-worker, Stan, who was a Christian. He was soft spoken, joyful and patient. He befriended me, answered my questions as best he could, and invited me to the lunchtime Bible study he led at work, and to his church.

I attended his church for a couple of months. Then came Good Friday. I remember how the Pastor said that this world was dying in its dirty, rotten and stinking sin while Jesus died on the cross to pay the penalty for sin. He gave the congregation an invitation to accept Jesus as Savior. After six years of Bible reading and generally searching for meaning in my life, I felt that I knew too much too refute Jesus' existence and ministry. I accepted the invitation. That was April 1, 1988.

In August 1988 I went with eight other people from the church's singles group to Montreal, Canada. We spent a week working alongside Pastor Bruce Muirhead, his wife, Claire, and daughter Lynne-Marie. Bruce was planting a new church in his community and used us as his arms and legs to go door-to-door to get the message out.

What stood out most from that week was how this little family of three opened their home to this stranger from Long Island, New York. They demonstrated the love and hospitality of God in such a real and tangible way. For six years I read about God's love. In that one week I experienced God's love fully.

As time passed I not only continued going on the annual week-long mission trip to Montreal, but I also went to Ireland (1991) and Ukraine (1992). Ukraine was special because our team went seven months after Communism fell and the Soviet Union broke apart. The spiritual hunger for God among the people was insatiable. We could not hand out New Testaments in the Russian language fast enough.

Closer to home my mother was battling cancer. For five years (1987-1992) she endured operations, treatments and many emotional highs and lows. After she died in November 1992 I experienced God's comfort during the grieving process. Joshua 1:9 read,

"Have I not commanded you? Be strong and courageous. Do not be terrified; do not be discouraged, for the LORD your God will be with you wherever you go" (NIV). I heard a song that put that verse to music and that song became my rock to hold onto.

In August 1993 I resigned from my job at a local aerospace company, packed my things and moved to Chicago, Illinois, to attend the Moody Bible Institute to earn a Master of Arts in Biblical Studies. My faith was challenged because I had to research to prove the Bible's authenticity. Was the Bible true? What was the evidence? Can the Bible be trusted? Is it a book written by men that is full of myths, fables, fairytales and legends? Taking the time to objectively weigh the evidence of the Bible's truth strengthened my faith.

On November 5, 1994, soon after my 31st birthday, I met the woman who would permanently change my life. Lisa Weinstein was from the Chicagoland area and a Jewish believer in Jesus just like me. The more we talked the more convinced I was that she was the woman I would marry. Naturally, she needed more convincing! Once convinced we were married on November 4, 1995.

Since then we have had our joys and our struggles. Our marriage started off rocky as we received a crash course in dying to ourselves. It was a difficult time learning how to blend and partner. The Lord needed to shave off the rough edges from both of us.

Our greatest joys were born in 2000 and 2003. Deborah and Rebekah have given us more joy than we could ever have imagined. And being parents has taught us how to show unconditional love to our girls just as God unconditionally loves His children in Jesus.

Over the years Lisa and I have served in various ministries at our church. We have served with children and led small group Bible studies. It's a joy contributing to the body of Christ in whatever measure we can.

The Lord faithfully provided employment for me while enabling Lisa to be a stay-at-home mom. I'm currently working at the Illinois division of that same aerospace company where I worked on Long Island, while Lisa stays at home and keeps everything (and everyone) organized. This has provided peace and stability for all of us.

I trust this brief overview has given you some insights into my life and journey. May the Lord bless you abundantly as you study His Word!

How to Use This Book

If you made it through reading my story of how I came to faith in Jesus, then you are ready to understand who this book is for and how to use it.

Psalm 119 is broken out into 22 sections with eight verses each. I will use these sections as daily devotions/meditations/ thoughts to highlight one specific theme. The intent is for the reader to use this as a daily quiet time while staying within the context of the entire psalm for one month of working days. This will help ignite the discipline of reading and studying God's Word daily and meditating upon its meaning.

Psalm 119 is a self-contained chapter in the longest book of the Bible. Each day you will remain in Psalm 119. In other devotionals you may jump around from Joshua to Acts to Haggai to John to Proverbs all in a span of 1 week. There is no consistency in that type of method.

Whenever I have the privilege of leading a Bible study I always focus on 4 essential elements to highlight the context. By way of review Psalm 119 consists of the following:

Author:	King David, Daniel or Ezra
Date:	1000 BC - 550 BC
Original Audience:	Nation of Israel
Major Theme:	The Supremacy of God's Word

Regardless of who the original author of this psalm was, it is quite apparent that he was very passionate about God's word. He was not interested in robotic religion or mechanical obedience. Rather, he surrendered his whole heart and soul to God, the One who made heaven and earth and gave humanity the perfect law to follow.

Feel free to repeat this study to gain new insights previously missed. Studying God's Word should never become stale nor boring. When you encounter a dry patch, continue to press forward and allow the Lord to work His truths into you and then through you for His glory. Apply your newfound discipline to other books and chapters in the Scriptures.

May this book be used as a tool for you to attain a delight in knowing, loving and serving the Lord with all of your heart, soul, mind and strength.

Day 1

Admit it

Blessed are the undefiled in the way,
who walk in the law of the LORD!
Blessed are those who keep
His testimonies, who seek Him
with the whole heart!
They also do no iniquity;
they walk in His ways.
You have commanded us to keep
Your precepts diligently.
Oh, that my ways were directed
to keep Your statutes!
Then I would not be ashamed, when
I look into all Your commandments.
I will praise You with uprightness of heart,
when I learn Your righteous judgments.
I will keep Your statutes; oh,
do not forsake me utterly!

Psalm 119:1 - 8

What kind of person do you admire and look up to? The celebrity, professional athlete, business person or politician who performs their vocation with excellence yet whose personal life is far from pure? Are you willing to overlook their flaws while admiring the results of their professional vocations?

The writer of Psalm 119 admired those people who remained undefiled, or pure, because they walked in the law of the LORD, kept His testimonies and sought Him with the whole heart (vv 1, 2). These are the kind of people who seem to radiate genuine goodness, kindness and encouragement whenever you're around them. Why is this? Because these people do no iniquity and choose to walk in God's ways. In other words, their lives are not marked by sinful living and behavior. They are the real deal.

A transition takes place in v. 4 as the psalmist addressed the LORD personally as "You". It is a life changing transition when we go from talking about the LORD conceptually in the theoretical and begin applying His principles to our lives in the practical. Are you ready and willing to make that transition?

The heart of this section is found in vv. 5, 6. It is here that the psalmist admitted his longing to keep God's perfect ways while being utterly incapable of doing so. Humility is a rapidly fading characteristic in all people today, believers and unbelievers alike. It's time to admit that we don't know it all. Furthermore, it's time to admit that the God of the Bible does know it all and prove it by letting Him take control of our hearts and lives.

Once we admit our complete inadequacy in following God's perfect law, the ability to freely express praise comes quite naturally. The burden is lifted and replaced by a hunger to know God better (v. 7). Praise is the natural result of learning more about the LORD and His ways.

Finally, the commitment is made to keep the LORD's statutes (v. 8). The psalmist is more concerned with receiving God's favor than anything else. Are we? When was the last time we truly compared ourselves against God's perfect character and equally perfect Word? And cared about it? Let's admit our sin (falling short of God's perfect standard) and fall at His feet in humble surrender and brokenness. He's more than willing to shower you with His mercy and grace.

Please, add your thoughts:

Day 2

Pure in Heart

How can a young man cleanse his way?
By taking heed according to Your word.
With my whole heart I have
sought You. Oh, let me not wander
from Your commandments!
Your word I have hidden in my heart,
that I might not sin against You.
Blessed are You, O LORD!
Teach me Your statutes.
With my lips I have declared all
the judgments of Your mouth.
I have rejoiced in the way of Your
testimonies, as much as in all riches.
I will meditate on Your precepts,
and contemplate Your ways.
I will delight myself in Your statutes;
I will not forget Your word.

Psalm 119:9 - 16

What kind of influences do you allow into your life? Are they the ones that leave you feeling filthy, soiled and violated? Or are they influences that leave you feeling clean with a clear conscience?

The writer of Psalm 119 did not consider purity a lost cause as many do today. Rather, he asked, "How can a young man cleanse his way?" (v. 9a). His answer? "By taking heed according to Your word" (v. 9b). He recognized that obeying God's Word was the only means by which he could live a God honoring life. (By the way, this is the first of twelve occurrences that the verse "according to Your word" appears in this Psalm. Keep an eye out for it).

Notice the absolute surrender the psalmist demonstrated towards God's Word. He had no shame in seeking God with his whole heart (v. 10a). Nor is there any sign of shame in his desire to not wander from His commandments (v. 10b). Rather, the psalmist resolved to hide God's Word in his heart so that he would not sin against Him (v. 11). Once His Word is allowed to reside within the heart of a teachable person, then the outer person will reflect a genuine devotion to God. That's the essential difference between long-term heart transformation versus short-term self-willed outward behavioral modification.

In our case, who do our family, friends, coworkers and neighbors see us living for? God and His ways? Or our own go nowhere selfish interests and desires?

The psalmist rejoiced that the LORD alone was able to keep him pure in all ways; thought, speech and action. He wanted to be taught the LORD's statutes (v. 12) so that he could turn around and be able to teach others (v. 13). This caused him to rejoice in the LORD's ways and place them as his top priority for life (v. 14). Studying, believing and applying God's truth so that it produced godly living became his greatest joy. Is it yours? Or do you derive greater pleasure with your numerous distractions? The choice is laid out for us each and everyday.

Last of all, the psalmist committed himself to meditating on the LORD's precepts, contemplating His ways, delighting in His statutes and not forgetting His word (vv. 15, 16). These verses are worth memorizing as they emphasize 4 basic truths about God's word:

1. Read it.
2. Study it.
3. Believe it.
4. Apply it.

The study of God's word breathes life into the soul who is humble, teachable and hungry to grow in His grace and knowledge. It should never be confined to a mere intellectual exercise.

How much time do you spend each day hiding God's word in your heart? What kind of results do you see in your life as a result of the time you spend reading (or not reading) your Bible? Is your life marked by purity?

"This is pure and undefiled religion in the sight of our God and Father...to keep oneself unstained by the world" (James 1:27, NASV).

Please, add your thoughts:

Day 3

A Servant's Prayer

Deal bountifully with Your servant,
that I may live and keep Your word.
Open my eyes, that I may see
wondrous things from Your law.
I am a stranger in the earth; do not
hide Your commandments from me.
My soul breaks with longing for
Your judgments at all times.
You rebuke the proud - the cursed, who
stray from Your commandments.
Remove from me reproach and contempt,
for I have kept Your testimonies.
Princes also sit and speak against me, but
Your servant meditates on Your statutes.
Your testimonies also are my
delight and my counselors.

Psalm 119:17 - 24

What do you think of when you hear the word servant? Someone who is at the mercy of a cruel master? Someone who has no freedom? A human piece of property? Merriam-Webster simply defines a servant as "one who serves others."

In God's economy there is no higher calling than to be His servant. The psalmist recognized his responsibility as being one who is under the authority of the LORD. He embraced servanthood so that he could live and keep God's word (v.17). He further showed his dependence upon the LORD by asking for his eyes to be opened to wondrous things from His law (v. 18). He knew that power to serve came from God, not simply by using his own will power.

Have you ever felt out of place being in a different location or among an unfamiliar group of people? Or both? The psalmist did as he referred to himself as a stranger on the earth (v. 19a). His single-minded devotion, service and living for God placed him among the minority of people in his day. Yet his hunger for God was much stronger than living for the things and accolades of this world. He belonged to God who gave him life through His commandments (v. 19b). He continually hungered to be led by God's law and was unashamed about it (v. 20).

It is comforting to know that God is just and punishes the proud and arrogant who brazenly rebel against His ways (v. 21). Why was the psalmist comforted by this thought? He had been the subject of reproach and contempt for keeping God's testimonies by the well known people of his day (vv.22, 23a). Yet he did not care. He continued to meditate on God's statutes (v. 23b) and was delighted to be counseled by His testimonies (v. 24). Regardless of the opposition the psalmist stayed the servant course with God. He chose to obey God at all times in all ways. Do you? Why or why not?

Remember the declaration of the greatest servant of all (Jesus) who said, "For even the Son of Man did not come to be served, but to serve, and to give His life a ransom for many" (Mark 10:45).

Please, add your thoughts:

Day 4
Rock Bottom

My soul clings to the dust; revive
me according to Your word.
I have declared my ways, and You have
answered me; teach me Your statutes.
Make me understand the way of
Your precepts; so shall I meditate
on Your wonderful works.
My soul melts from heaviness;
strengthen me according to Your word.
Revive me from the way of lying,
and grant me Your law graciously.
I have chosen the way of truth; Your
judgments I have laid before me.
I cling to Your testimonies; O
LORD, do not put me to shame!
I will run the course of Your
commandments, for You
shall enlarge my heart.

Psalm 119:25 - 32

What does it take to completely discourage and dishearten you? Losing your job? Poor health of a loved one, friend or yourself? Tight finances? No positive family support? No friends? The never-ending stresses of life?

The psalmist hit rock bottom as his soul clung to the dust (v. 25a). His soul was completely drained of hope. Where did he go to be revived? Back to God's word (v. 25b). The psalmist expected the LORD to come through for him as He had previously (v. 26a). He longed to be taught more of the LORD's ways as his only means of attaining hope (v. 26b).

What thoughts comfort you in times of distress and trouble? The psalmist meditated on the "wonderful works" of God (v. 27). Like what? Maybe creation, the Exodus of the children of Israel from Egypt, Moses giving Israel the Ten Commandments, the promise of the Messiah through David's line or maybe other specific things done in his life that only God can receive credit for. Meditating on God's greatness and "wonderful works" is the first step toward receiving hope.

The psalmist's battle with depression was not over yet as his soul melted with heaviness (v. 28a). Yet he sought strength from God's word (v. 28b). He looked outside of himself and toward the One who alone is able to give him strength to carry on (v. 28b).

The next thing the psalmist did was to confess his sin of lying and have it replaced by God's truth (vv. 29, 30). Self-willed efforts at change only last a short period of time and ultimately falter. God's word forces us to make a choice of relying upon our own strength or His. To follow Him or reject Him. What choice do you make on an everyday basis?

Rather than cling to the dust (v. 25) the psalmist chose to cling to God's testimonies (v. 31a). He realized that his only hope of overcoming despair was to cling to God's word much in the same way a drowning person clings to a life preserver while unable to swim in a deep and dangerous body of water. He expected victory and not shame in choosing the LORD (v. 31b).

Finally, the psalmist was committed to "run the course" of life by obediently following God and His ways. He knew that only the LORD provided strength and courage which enables weak and broken people to complete the race (v. 32). He chose to rely upon the LORD's strength and wisdom to uphold him during this incredibly difficult period in his life.

When you are broken, whose ways do you choose? Where do you go for wisdom? Whose strength do you rely upon?

Please, add your thoughts:

Day 5
Status Quo? No!

Teach me, O LORD, the way of Your
statutes, and I shall keep it to the end.
Give me understanding, and I
shall keep Your law; indeed, I shall
observe it with my whole heart.
Make me walk in the path of Your
commandments, for I delight in it.
Incline my heart to Your testimonies,
and not to covetousness.
Turn away my eyes from
looking at worthless things, and
revive me in Your way.
Establish Your word to Your servant,
who is devoted to fearing You.
Turn away my reproach which I dread,
for Your judgments are good.
Behold, I long for Your precepts;
revive me in Your righteousness.

Psalm 119:33 - 40

What do you think when some people claim, "I have a relationship with God?" Do you think they're from another planet? Have they gone over the edge? Or have they truly tapped into something (or Someone) who has the power to bring about true change, peace and joy into one's life?

The psalmist's desire was to be taught the way of God's statutes and gain understanding (vv. 33a, 34a). Why? So that he could keep them to the end and observe them with his whole heart (vv. 33b, 34b). He set his own *status quo* agenda aside with its predetermined bias and outcome. Instead, his greatest desire was to apply the LORD's word as opposed to filing away religious facts or spiritual information. He desired that elusive change of life that can only be born through a genuine relationship with the God of the universe, not mere religious observance.

Taking the first step away from the *status quo* is always filled with uncertainty. But as the psalmist pointed out, his greatest delight was walking (or living) in the path of God's commandments (v. 35). All it took was complete dissatisfaction with the *status quo* and the courage to do something about it.

How much time, money and energy do we waste coveting worthless things instead of finding contentment with God, the One who fashioned us? We could all save ourselves a lot of unnecessary pain and disappointment by allowing God's word to revive us and placing our life focus upon Him where it truly belongs (vv. 36, 37).

To whom are we devoted? Is there anyone or anything you truly fear? Unless we imitate the psalmist's example by surrendering our lives to the LORD and His ways we will forever be stuck on a treadmill of a joyless, mediocre life. Crave His presence, obey His word, serve Him with reverence (v. 38).

Up to this point the psalmist sought the LORD in order to be changed from within. Now the psalmist is asking the LORD to change his circumstances by removing the reproach he dreaded. He completely placed his trust in the hands of Him whose judgments are good (v. 39).

Finally, the psalmist expressed his longing for the LORD's precepts to revive him (v. 40). He was no longer satisfied with the results of a *status quo* life. He knew that it was time to lay aside his own desires and bias and move toward God's word and character.

Do you want to buck the *status quo* of a mediocre existence? Are you willing to

23

discard the *status quo* and begin to live a fresh, dynamic and renewed life with the LORD in charge? The way to buck the *status quo* is to be humble, teachable, and willing to let God change you on His terms. It's your turn to choose.

Please, add your thoughts:

Day 6

10 Benefits from God's Word

Let Your mercies come also to me, O LORD
- Your salvation according to Your word.
So shall I have an answer for him who
reproaches me, for I trust in Your word.
And take not the word of truth
utterly out of my mouth, for I have
hoped in Your ordinances.
So shall I keep Your law
continually, forever and ever.
And I will walk at liberty, for
I seek Your precepts.
I will speak of Your testimonies also
before kings, and will not be ashamed.
And I will delight myself in Your
commandments, which I love.
My hands also will I lift up to Your
commandments, which I love, and
I will meditate on Your statutes.

Psalm 119:41 - 48

What values do you possess? How do they guide your life? What kind of person are you as a result? God's word transforms us from the inside out and yields great benefits for those who live by it. The following 10 benefits from today's passage are but a sample. Maybe you can find more.

1. **God's Mercy** (v. 41a). It all starts here. Without God's mercy nothing else matters. His mercy can be defined as "God not giving us the punishment we deserve due to our rebellion against Him." His mercy should make us stop and think of how awesome He is. His ability to show us pity when we're in distress should bring us comfort and security. But God's mercy should never be taken for granted. One day it will run out on those who continually rebel against His authority and that of His Son, Jesus Christ.

2. **Salvation** (v. 41b). In this context the psalmist is referring to being delivered from reproach.

3. **Wisdom** (v. 42). When confronted with a persistent and troublesome situation, the psalmist trusted God's word for guidance. God led, he followed. Is that your standard way of living?

4. **Hope** (v. 43). Hope is indispensable. With it there's light and life. Without it there's darkness and death. The psalmist received hope from God's word as he endured his difficult trial. God's word is that rock solid and firm foundation which provides hope, peace and security for those honest enough to admit their need. Make time each day to spend time in His word and watch your hope grow!

5. **Obedience** (v. 44). As a result of receiving God's mercy and the previous benefits, the psalmist made the conscious choice to keep God's "law continually, forever and ever." He made the commitment to obey the LORD wholeheartedly instead of living a double life. Obedience brings God's blessing while rebellious disobedience delivers God's curse (Deut. 28). Choose this day whom you will serve (Josh. 24:15).

6. **Liberty** (v. 45). Embracing the power of God through His word sets us free from the enslavement of sin and its consequences. We're no longer bound to blindly yield

ourselves to sin's power. Temptations will continue to present themselves in various ways, but in Christ we have the power to say "no" to sin and "yes" to God.

7. **Boldness** (v. 46). The psalmist was ready to speak to others on God's behalf. And he was willing to do it boldly without shame. When those rare opportunities arise to tell others about the LORD and His working in your life, "be ready in season and out of season" (2 Tim. 4:2).

8. **Joy** (v. 47). The result of all the psalmist's study, meditation and application of God's word is being filled with joy. Joy is also a fruit of the Spirit (Gal. 5:22), the outward evidence of a life consumed with God.

9. **Praise** (v. 48a). The psalmist lifted his hands to God's commandments. That outward expression of praise reflected the inner thanksgiving and gratitude the psalmist had for how God worked in his life. How often do you give praise to God for who He is and what He has done for your life?

10. **Desire to Study** (v. 48b). Finally, the psalmist committed himself to meditate on God's statutes. His continued desire to study God's word bore the fruit of a deeper and more intimate relationship with his Creator.

The more you hang around someone the more you become like that someone. That was the psalmist's deepest desire; to properly reflect the character of the LORD.

Please, add your thoughts:

Day 7

Reflections from Long Island

Remember the word to Your servant, upon
which You have caused me to hope.
This is my comfort in my affliction,
for Your word has given me life.
The proud have me in great derision,
yet I do not turn aside from Your law.
I remembered Your judgments of old,
O LORD, and have comforted myself.
Indignation has taken hold of me because
of the wicked, who forsake Your law.
Your statutes have been my songs
in the house of my pilgrimage.
I remember Your name in the night,
O LORD, and I keep Your law.
This has become mine, because
I kept Your precepts.

Psalm 119:49 - 56

Current Introduction:

The following excerpts were written on July 3, 1999 from my childhood bedroom on Long Island. My wife Lisa and I were on vacation and visited family and friends. This entry was my first attempt at commenting on today's passage as I reflected on my life. Note that I interspersed current thoughts within the original.

Original Introduction:

I write this from my old bedroom while on vacation. It was here that I read the Bible for 6 years (ages 18-24) until I accepted Jesus as my Messiah. It was also here in this room that I used to take refuge with music, TV or sleep when home life was rough and joyless. Things have wonderfully changed in my life since those days and I'm forever grateful!

"As the LORD is ever so faithful it seems as though this section of Scripture relates to where I am now while causing me to remember where I came from.

Living here never inspired hope except to get away to someplace better. Yet the psalmist reflects on the LORD's word which caused him to hope (v. 49). Our hope is not restricted for this life only but carries over to the life to come.

God's word provides two things:
1. It provides "comfort in...affliction."
2. It gives life (v. 50).

Reading the word during those early years gave me comfort and hope for a new life. I knew that life was not meant to be lived in joyless darkness but rather to be enjoyed and savored with anticipation."

Who do you cling to when dark times come upon you? The psalmist suffered mocking and scoffing at the hands of arrogant people, but he did not turn aside from God's law (v. 51). He remembered the LORD's judgments of old (possibly the Flood, the Exodus from Egypt, other personal victories in his life for which God can get credit) and was comforted (v. 52). The LORD was his hope, comfort and life as He was mine in my younger days. Is He yours?

Let's face it; arrogant people are a burden and weigh us down. Those who brazenly forsake the LORD and His ways can easily annoy you. "As my faith grew I learned to praise the LORD while understanding that

35

this life is just a place I'm passing through. My pilgrimage has taken me from darkness to light, blindness to sight. The journey's not over but I'm very grateful for the progress He has led me to experience" (vv. 53, 54).

When life turns into extended periods of night, to whom do you turn for help? Family? Friends? Substances? Work? Religion? Study God's word and meditate on it. You will find comfort, hope and life. And by embracing the LORD you will find how hope, comfort and life in Him become the very fiber of your being.

"What has become mine? Hope, comfort and life. The LORD's word has provided me with hope for the future as well as the present; comfort in times of stress and affliction; new life which I could never have attained through my own efforts and works. It's all praise to Jesus as Lord for the new life He brings!

Remembering what the LORD has done is a great exercise in recharging one's faith. Every believer should always take the time to reflect every now and then. Thank you LORD for the opportunity to do so in this place!" (v. 56).

Embrace the LORD, study His word and receive the hope, comfort and life that await those who completely place their trust in Him alone.

Please, add your thoughts:

Day 8

A Repentant Heart

You are my portion, O LORD; I have
said that I would keep Your words.
I entreated Your favor with my
whole heart; be merciful to me
according to Your word.
I thought about my ways, and turned
my feet to Your testimonies.
I made haste, and did not delay
to keep Your commandments.
The cords of the wicked have bound
me, but I have not forgotten Your law.
At midnight I will rise to give thanks to
You, because of Your righteous judgments.
I am a companion of all who fear You,
and of those who keep Your precepts.
The earth, O LORD, is full of Your
mercy; teach me Your statutes.

Psalm 119:57 - 64

What does it take to bring about permanent change to your life? Some sort of heavy-duty crisis such as a job loss? Accident? Health crisis to someone close to you or yourself? Change is never easy. Even to the Christian. Yet it is absolutely necessary if one truly desires to grow in their faith.

No matter how strong or weak one's relationship with the LORD is, it is a necessary step to acknowledge that He is our portion and we are subject to His words. Follow the example of the psalmist by acknowledging that He is always enough (v. 57).

The next thing the psalmist did was to entreat the LORD's favor with his whole heart and ask for mercy according to His word (v. 58). The psalmist opened up his whole heart and held nothing back. He exhibited genuine transparency with the willingness to change.

Here is the perfect picture of repentance, "I thought about my ways, and turned my feet to Your testimonies. I made haste, and did not delay to keep Your commandments" (vv.59, 60). When was the last time you seriously took a look at your life in the light of Scripture? Can you honestly say that you have desired to walk faithfully with the LORD? Whose direction do you most frequently follow? Yours or the LORD's? The psalmist compared his ways to God's and found himself lacking. He changed direction quickly and got onto God's road. He did not wait for a heavenly sign. He knew what he needed to do and did not delay. Take a moment to evaluate your journey with the LORD. Ask Jesus to forgive your sin and change your heart. Only then will you be able to faithfully and joyfully obey Him.

Although the psalmist repented of his sin and changed the direction of his life, he still contended with wicked people. Sometimes circumstances do not change. That's why it is so important for our commitment to God to be from the heart and not just the head (v. 61).

One way to show true repentance is to demonstrate gratitude toward the LORD for who He is and what He has done in your life. Thankfulness makes us pause to remember that it's the LORD and His power alone that changes hearts, lives and direction. Any time of day or night is the right time to offer Him praise and thanksgiving (v. 62).

Another way to demonstrate commitment to the LORD and His ways is to befriend those who love and fear Him on the same level as you do. Together you can keep each other faithful, encouraged and accountable during life's ups and downs (v. 63).

Finally, the psalmist recognized the LORD's mercy everywhere (v. 64). How? He realized that he was given another chance instead of receiving deserved judgment. Repentance involves coming to God who delights in showing mercy and forgiveness. Once forgiven continue to demonstrate a humble and teachable spirit by learning more about the LORD and His ways. Be a lifelong student and your life will be forever changed for the better!

Please, add your thoughts:

Day 9

The Benefits of Affliction

You have dealt well with Your servant,
O LORD, according to Your word.
Teach me good judgment and knowledge,
for I believe Your commandments.
Before I was afflicted I went astray,
but now I keep Your word.
You are good, and do good;
teach me Your statutes.
The proud have forged a lie
against me, but I will keep Your
precepts with my whole heart.
Their heart is as fat as grease,
but I delight in Your law.
It is good for me that I have been
afflicted, that I may learn Your statutes.
The law of Your mouth is better to me
than thousands of coins of gold and silver.

Psalm 119:65 - 72

When was the last time you dealt with genuine pain, heartache, suffering or sorrow? Are you going through any of this now? Do you wonder where is the LORD at this time in your life? Usually it is through the pain He speaks the loudest.

The psalmist had no complaints about how the LORD dealt with him. In fact, he thought the LORD dealt well with him "according to Your word" (v.65). Furthermore, he desired the LORD to teach him good judgment and knowledge (v. 66). Why? Having good judgment and knowledge would enable him (and us) to deal with life's pain when it arrives at our doorstep.

The psalmist's honesty is refreshing. He freely admitted that he went astray. However, instead of using his confession as a means of rejoicing in rebellion as is so common in today's culture, he returned to the LORD and pledged to keep His word. And then he praised the LORD as One who is good and does good (vv. 67, 68). The good character of the LORD was never questioned during this period of affliction.

Why does the LORD allow or cause affliction in our lives? For the Christian affliction is proof that God disciplines those He loves (Proverbs 3:11, 12; Hebrews 12: 5, 6). For the non-Christian affliction is a wake-up call to turn from our sins (repentance) and embrace the forgiveness that only the resurrected Jesus offers. The goal of affliction is to give birth to humility and a teachable heart. Are we willing to obey His call to live obediently by His statutes?

How do you react when you discover that lies are being spread about you? Vengeance? Correct the record? The psalmist made no threats or proclamations of getting even. Instead, he determined to keep the LORD's precepts with his whole heart while contrasting the hearts of his adversaries ("fat as grease") as impenetrable and unfeeling (vv. 69, 70).

Finally, the psalmist found good in affliction. Affliction taught him to learn God's statutes as he considered their worth better to him than riches (vv. 71, 72).

Decision time has come. What actions will you choose when times of affliction come? Will you choose to wait on the LORD and embrace the hope He offers through His word? Or will you embrace bitterness and the temporary good feeling of revenge? God may or may not change the circumstances. But He will always change us as long as we allow Him to.

Please, add your thoughts:

Day 10

What is God Like?

Your hands have made and fashioned
me; give me understanding that I
may learn Your commandments.
Those who fear You will be glad
when they see me, because I
have hoped in Your word.
I know, O LORD, that Your judgments
are right, and that in faithfulness
You have afflicted me.
Let, I pray, Your merciful kindness
be my comfort, according to
Your word to Your servant.
Let Your tender mercies come to me, that
I may live; for Your law is my delight.
Let the proud be ashamed, for they
treated me wrongfully with falsehood;
but I will meditate on Your precepts.
Let those who fear You turn to me,
those who know Your testimonies.
Let my heart be blameless regarding Your
statutes, that I may not be ashamed.

Psalm 119:73 - 80

What is God like? What attributes do you think He possess? Take a few moments to reread the scripture passage and note the characteristics you find before you continue with today's reading.

The first attribute of God is that of Almighty Creator. The psalmist is not embarrassed to declare that God "fashioned" him (v. 73a). He is not embarrassed to voice his joys, sorrows, struggles and burdens to an actual Person who knows him better than he knows himself.

A second attribute is God's omniscience, or all-knowing (v. 73b). The psalmist asked the LORD to grant him "understanding...to learn" God's commandments. Only an all-knowing Creator can empower and equip His creation to understand Him and His ways.

If we truly believe that God is an all-knowing Creator, then we should exhibit a healthy "fear" of Him. We can fear God in a healthy way and "be glad" about it (v. 74). He's more powerful and awesome than anyone or anything else. How can we not fear Him?

A third attribute is a comforting one: Faithfulness. God is faithful (v. 75). He can be trusted and counted upon. He is always there. He never leaves nor forsakes those who love and fear Him.

Fourth is mercy (vv. 76, 77). Despite ignorant misrepresentations that the LORD delights in demonstrating anger and wrath to a rebellious world, He is forever merciful and kind toward those who earnestly seek Him. His true delight is showing mercy and kindness to us who don't deserve it because of our sin. The end result for us is receiving comfort in our afflictions, peace in our trials and a delight in His presence.

Implied in v. 78 is the fifth attribute of justice. The psalmist voiced his certain conviction that a future time is coming for those who rebel against God and His law to be ashamed. The mercy of God is extended to all during each one's lifetime but only continues in those who love and obey Him.

The psalmist's strength and support are found in two areas: 1) Meditating on the LORD's precepts (v. 78b). 2) Being with other God-fearing people (v. 79). The idea is that the congregation is to be strengthened and supported by those who hold the same convictions and have also gone through similar trials. No one needs to go through life alone.

Finally, the psalmist's heart desire is to be blameless (v. 80). This is a reflection of the last of God's attributes in this section:

Holiness. Holiness is the attribute that separates the LORD from us and all others. He alone is completely pure and blameless. His desire is for those who follow Him to pursue that same quality in our lives. He is the only One who has the ability to make our hearts blameless and pure. Is that your desire?

Please, add your thoughts:

Day 11

Faithful in Desperate Times

My soul faints for Your salvation,
but I hope in Your word.
My eyes fail from searching Your word,
saying, "When will You comfort me?"
For I have become like a wineskin in
smoke, yet I do not forget Your statutes.
How many are the days of Your servant?
When will You execute judgment
on those who persecute me?
The proud have dug pits for me,
which is not according to Your law.
All Your commandments are faithful; they
persecute me wrongfully; help me!
They almost made an end of me on earth,
but I did not forsake Your precepts.
Revive me according to Your
lovingkindness, so that I may keep
the testimony of Your mouth.

Psalm 119:81 - 88

Have you ever been tempted to cast God aside when life became too tough? If so, did you follow through and give up on Him? Or did you continue following Him even though He seemed distant and silent?

The psalmist hit a wall. His strength was completely gone ("My soul faints..." v. 81a) and the crossroads arrived. His decision? "I hope in Your word" (v. 81b). Good start. But what happens when you can't seem to find comfort from God's word (v. 82)? Another crossroads. Do you bag and can His word? Or do you keep pressing on?

What is a "wineskin in smoke" (v. 83a)? It was a leather pouch designed to hold wine. If it dried up it cracked and leaked, thus spilling its contents and not fulfilling its original design. The psalmist felt dry, cracked and worn out. Life had leaked out of him. His response ? "Yet I do not forget Your statutes" (v. 83b). God's word continually gave him hope in the very midst of his trials.

Furthermore, the psalmist looked forward to the day when God's justice would be carried out in his lifetime against those who persecuted him (v. 84). Maybe he focused upon Deuteronomy 28, the familiar chapter that communicated God's blessing upon those who obeyed Him and curses upon those who disobeyed. God's promise of ultimate justice sparked hope for the psalmist to keep pressing on.

The opposition against the psalmist involved much more than slander and lies; his very life was in danger (vv. 85 - 87). His enemies "dug pits" (v. 85a) and "almost made an end" of him (v. 87). Despite these threats to his life, his basis of hope came from God, about whom he said, "all Your commandments are faithful" (v. 86a). His hope was found in seeking God's help (v. 86b) and he was careful not to forsake the LORD's precepts (v. 87b).

The psalmist sought a genuine revival in his spirit courtesy of the LORD's lovingkindness (v. 88a). Nothing less than God's genuine intervention into his life would do. He knew that only God has the power to provide peace during life's chaos, comfort in life's sorrows and security in life's storms. Revival does not originate from within. It originates from without through the LORD's abundant mercy and grace.

What's the purpose of revival?

1. Renews our commitment that only Jesus forgives people's sins through the shedding of His blood on the cross and His Resurrection.

2. Renews our commitment to fear God for who He really is. He is the Almighty Creator, not some politically correct, watered down version as He's commonly portrayed today.
3. Renews our courage to obey Him regardless of the cost.
4. Renews our perspective that one day Jesus will return to reward those who are His and punish those who rebel against Him.

Genuine revival produces the courage to obey God even when we don't feel like it. Don't accept imitations!

Please, add your thoughts:

Day 12

Our Eternal, Faithful Creator

Forever, O LORD, Your word
is settled in heaven.
Your faithfulness endures to all
generations; You established
the earth, and it abides.
They continue this day according to Your
ordinances, for all are Your servants.
Unless Your law had been my delight, I
would have perished in my affliction.
I will never forget Your precepts, for
by them You have given me life.
I am Yours, save me; for I have
sought Your precepts.
The wicked wait for me, to destroy me,
but I will consider Your testimonies.
I have seen the consummation of all
perfection, but Your commandment
is exceedingly broad.

Psalm 119:89 - 96

When was the last time you thought about how long forever is? If we lived for 100 years that would equal 36,525 days (including 25 leap years). As long as that may appear it is nothing when compared with eternity.

In today's passage the psalmist has shifted his perspective from the temporal to the eternal. He declared, "Forever, O LORD, Your word is settled in heaven" (v. 89). There is no end to forever. Jesus Himself said, "Heaven and earth will pass away, but My words will by no means pass away" (Mark 13:31). Have His words passed away? Hardly. Some 2,000 years later Jesus' words are as fresh, controversial, soul-piercing and life changing as ever. They are still here for all to see.

Not only is God's word eternal, His "faithfulness endures to all generations" (v. 90a). All generations includes biblical times right up to the present. Every nation. Every people group. God's faithfulness is always there. Have you recognized it in your life?

Next, the psalmist confidently declared the LORD as Creator (vv. 90b, 91). He is the

Designer and Sustainer of the world and all it contains. Creation serves the LORD, not the other way around.

The psalmist viewed the LORD as the eternal and faithful Creator. Therefore, he confidently placed his trust in God's word. God's word became his delight (v. 92), gave him life (v. 93) and saved him (v. 94). Only an eternal and faithful Creator can write a perfect book that is able to bring hope, meaning and purpose to people of every generation regardless of race, nationality or language.

Where do you place your hope and trust when that never-ending problem will not go away? For the psalmist it was in the LORD's testimonies (v. 95). He rejoiced in his eternal and faithful Creator. He observed that even perfection (or creation itself) had its limits. But God's word is "exceedingly broad" (v. 96) or without limit. It has no boundaries. It penetrates the hearts of all who embrace it.

There you have it. What's your choice? Rely upon your own ingenuity and scheming to overcome life's obstacles while achieving temporary satisfaction? Or place your whole-hearted trust in the eternal and faithful Creator of the universe who wrote a perfect book and gave His perfect Son to save people of all kinds from their sin? Where is your hope centered?

Please, add your thoughts:

Day 13

The Way of Wisdom

Oh, how I love Your law! It is
my meditation all the day.
You, through Your commandments,
make me wiser than my enemies;
for they are ever with me.
I have more understanding
than all my teachers, for Your
testimonies are my meditation.
I understand more than the ancients,
because I keep Your precepts.
I have restrained my feet from every
evil way, that I may keep Your way.
I have not departed from Your judgments,
for You Yourself have taught me.
How sweet are Your words to my taste,
sweeter than honey to my mouth!
Through Your precepts I get
understanding; therefore, I
hate every false way.

Psalm 119:97 - 104

Have you known people in your life who were academically intelligent but lacked common sense? How about those who were not the top in their class but exercised great sense and wisdom? What does it take to be a wise person?

In today's passage the psalmist highlighted three key elements that need to be exercised if one desires to become a person known for wisdom:

1) Meditate on God's Word. The psalmist loved God's law and it became his "meditation all the day" (v. 97). He had more than just a passing interest. God's word became his consuming passion. This is where he learned who God is and what He is like. The study of God's word became the focused study of his life.

2) Gain Understanding in God's Word. Paul encouraged Timothy, "Study to show thyself approved" (2 Tim. 3:15, KJV). The psalmist knew that understanding God's word led to becoming wise. He took the time to look not only at the words but also to contemplate their meaning (v. 98). Remember his counsel earlier from 119:15, 16? He meditated on God's precepts. He contemplated God's ways. He delighted himself in God's statutes and did not want to forget God's word.

Be intentional to take 15 minutes each day to read a portion of God's word in its context. Be still and quiet. Keep all distractions turned off. Over time you will find this discipline beginning to pay off. God's word will become abundant in your head and will begin to live in your heart as long as you're humble and teachable.

3) Obey God's Word. Why did the psalmist feel that he understood more than his teachers and the ancients (vv. 99, 100a)? Was he being arrogant? No. The difference between him and others was that he kept God's precepts (v. 100b). He exercised God-given self-control in order to remain obedient (v. 101). He was able to declare with a clear conscience, "I have not departed from Your judgments" (v. 102a).

Nothing brought the psalmist greater delight than God's word (v. 103). Why? Through the consistent and diligent study of God's word he gained understanding and learned to discern between truth and falsehood (v. 104). That's wisdom. Learning what God's word says and then doing it.

Is God's word your greatest desire and delight? Are you growing in your understanding of it? Are you obeying what it says? Take a few moments to answer these questions honestly.

Please, add your thoughts:

Day 14
No Matter What

Your word is a lamp to my feet
and a light to my path.
I have sworn and confirmed that I will
keep Your righteous judgments.
I am afflicted very much; revive me,
O LORD, according to Your word.
Accept, I pray, the freewill
offerings of my mouth, O LORD,
and teach me Your judgments.
My life is continually in my hand,
yet I do not forget Your law.
The wicked have laid a snare for me, yet
I have not strayed from Your precepts.
Your testimonies I have taken as
a heritage forever, for they are
the rejoicing of my heart.
I have inclined my heart to perform
Your statutes forever, to the very end.

Psalm 119:105 - 112

What does it take for you to make a solid commitment to change? A serious health crisis? Marriage falling apart? Poor financial decisions? What does it take for you to reach a point of saying, "I'm going to improve in this area no matter what"?

The psalmist decided to stick with God's word no matter what. He compared it to a "lamp to my feet and a light to my path" (v. 105). God's word provides enough illumination to keep us walking on a straight, smooth path. But it requires a commitment to stick with it. For example, when I drive on Interstate 80 from Chicago to Long Island I cannot see the Empire State Building 800 miles away. But if I continue to follow the right signs and not deviate from my course then I will eventually arrive at my destination. All it takes is the periodic appearance of a road sign to confirm my direction. The road sign for the Christian is God's word.

Check out the resolve of the psalmist to keep following the LORD no matter the suffering and affliction he endured (v. 107):

1. He swore and confirmed to keep God's righteous judgments (v. 106).
2. He freely gave praise to the LORD (v. 108a).
3. He desired to be taught God's word (v. 108b).
4. He never forgot God's law even though his life was continually at risk (v. 109).
5. He did not stray from the LORD's precepts (v. 110).
6. He consciously chose to obey the LORD forever (vv. 111a, 112).
7. His heart rejoiced over God's testimonies (v. 111b).

The psalmist did not use his affliction as an excuse to abandon his faith in the LORD. He suffered. He was hurting. But these trials made him see his need for the LORD's strength and wisdom all the more. He dug his feet into the foundation of God's word and said, "I will obey and follow You no matter what."

Read between the lines and look at the psalmist's heart. Despite his suffering he freely displayed a humble and teachable spirit. His desire to follow and cling to the LORD was stronger than ever.

Evaluate your own heart. Will you allow God's word to be a lamp to your feet and a light to your path no matter what?

Please, add your thoughts:

Day 15

God of Justice

I hate the double-minded,
but I love Your law.
You are my hiding place and my
shield; I hope in Your word.
Depart from me, you evildoers, for I will
keep the commandments of my God!
Uphold me according to Your word,
that I may live; and do not let
me be ashamed of my hope.
Hold me up, and I shall be safe, and I
shall observe Your statutes continually.
You reject all those who stray from Your
statutes, for their deceit is falsehood.
You put away all the wicked of
the earth like dross; therefore
I love Your testimonies.
My flesh trembles for fear of You, and
I am afraid of Your judgments.

Psalm 119:113 - 120

What does it take for you to long for justice? Attacks on your character? Someone slanders your spouse? Your children are bullied? A friend turns on you? You are the victim of a crime?

In this section the psalmist's patience toward his opponents has worn thin. "I hate the double-minded" (v. 113a). What is a double-minded person? Literally, one who is divided in heart or mind. A double-minded person gives equal validity to both the sacred and the profane. He lives in both worlds instead of committing to one. This person practices deceit. Nothing genuine emanates from him. Like a chameleon this person changes colors only to suit his own purposes and cares nothing for anyone else. A double-minded person is a hypocrite, untrustworthy, unreliable and unstable.

Conversely, the psalmist loved God's law (v. 113b). Why? He knew God's law was written by the only genuine, trustworthy, reliable and stable God of all. This confidence led the psalmist to refer to God as his hiding place and enabled him to place his trust in God's word (v. 114).

The psalmist considered double-minded people evil for he knew that they had the potential to steer him away from God's commandments (v. 115). He knew that hanging around double-minded people would cause him to stumble and get hurt.

The psalmist needed to be upheld according to God's word in order to 1) live, 2) have hope, 3) be safe (vv. 116, 117). Who do you have in your life that consistently provides all three benefits on a 24/7/365 basis?

What is the penalty for straying from God's statutes and practicing a lifetime of deceit and falsehood? Being rejected by the LORD. Double-minded people will eventually be exposed for what they truly are and pay the eternal price for it (v. 118).

The psalmist did not take vengeance into his own hands. He patiently waited for the LORD to ultimately judge his enemies and continued to rejoice in God's testimonies (v. 119). He knew that ultimately God had the last word toward "all the wicked of the earth."

Finally, the psalmist trusted the LORD to dispense perfect justice in His way and time. He demonstrated a healthy fear of the LORD. He knew that one day all of humanity will need to give an account to the Almighty Creator, Sustainer and Judge of all the universe. Nothing will remain hidden from Him on that final day.

How are we living our lives? Are we choosing to live with a healthy fear of God and demonstrate it by following His ways? Or are we double-minded people completely consumed with our own self-interests and deceiving ourselves? Be honest with yourself.

Please, add your thoughts:

Day 16

A Servant's Heart

I have done justice and righteousness;
do not leave me with my oppressors.
Be surety to Your servant for good;
do not let the proud oppress me.
My eyes fail from seeking Your
salvation and Your righteous word.
Deal with Your servant according to Your
mercy, and teach me Your statutes.
I am Your servant; give me understanding
that I may know Your testimonies.
It is time for You to act, O LORD, for
they have regarded Your law as void.
Therefore, I love Your commandments
more than gold, yes, than fine gold!
Therefore, all Your precepts
concerning all things I consider to
be right; I hate every false way.

Psalm 119:121 - 128

Have you ever been given a task to complete only to encounter consistent obstacles and roadblocks? As tempting as it is to quit you continue to press forward even though the progress is slow and painstaking.

The psalmist continued to find himself in that very familiar position. His desire was to live a just and righteous life but his steps were impeded by those who oppressed him (vv. 121, 122). Trying to live a godly life in an ungodly world invites that type of pressure. Can you sense his frustration and relate to his plight?

What did the psalmist do? Did he turn his back on God and reject Him? Did the constant presence of opposition defeat him? By no means!

Notice that the psalmist referred to himself as "Your servant" three times (vv. 122, 124, 125). This was a title he held in high esteem. He was glad to be identified as a servant of the LORD even though opposition was part of the deal.

As a servant the psalmist sought comfort from the LORD, not from anyone nor anywhere else. His eyes failed from seeking the LORD's salvation and righteous word (v. 123); he sought the LORD's mercy (v. 124a); he desired to be taught the LORD's statutes (v. 124b); he wanted understanding to live according to God's ways (v. 125). Why? This servant demonstrated a true love and loyalty toward his Master during the tough times. He knew that his only strength was found by holding fast to his Master, not running away.

It grieved the psalmist's heart to see his enemies regard God's law as void (v. 126). He was anxious to see the LORD vindicate Himself and dispense justice. But the LORD acts on His timetable, not ours. Waiting upon the LORD is a standard discipline in the Christian life (see Isaiah 40:31).

Finally, the psalmist's passion for God's commandments far exceeded anything that this world regarded as valuable (v. 127). He considered God's ways to be right when compared with the world's lies and deceptions (v. 128). As a result his convictions grew stronger for upholding God's precepts. And as a servant, his allegiance grew stronger for his Master. That was the conscious choice he made when seeing the contrast between God's holy ways and the ways of the world.

What choice are you making? Would you rather "be a doorkeeper in the house of my God than dwell in the tents of wickedness"? (Psalm 84:10).

Please, add your thoughts:

Day 17

10 Reminders to Keep Pressing On

Your testimonies are wonderful;
therefore, my soul keeps them.
The entrance of Your word gives light;
it gives understanding to the simple.
I opened my mouth and panted, for
I longed for Your commandments.
Look upon me and be merciful
to me, as Your custom is toward
those who love Your name.
Direct my steps by Your word, and let
no iniquity have dominion over me.
Redeem me from the oppression of
man, that I may keep Your precepts.
Make Your face shine upon Your
servant, and teach me Your statutes.
Rivers of water run down from my eyes,
because men do not keep Your law.

Psalm 119:129 - 136

E very now and then we need reminders to keep pressing forward when we hit a wall. We were faithful to reach this point but now our spiritual fuel is running low. A fresh fill-up of encouragement is needed.

Sometimes it's that way living the Christian life. We need to be reminded of who God is and how He is willing to change our hearts and lives when we allow Him. Here are 10 reminders of why we need to keep pressing on with God and His word.

1) **Joy** (v.129a). The psalmist found God's "testimonies wonderful." They were the source of his joy and delight. Despite the opposition he faced from wicked people, God's word provided joy to his life.

2) **Desire to Obey** (v.129b). It's much easier to stay the course when your heart is in it. Find joy in God and His word and then set your mind on obeying Him. As you trust and obey God and His word you will experience joy that this world cannot make counterfeit.

3) **Understanding** (v. 130). Light chases away darkness the instant it shines. God's word "gives understanding to the simple." It sharpens minds that were previously dulled by this world's philosophy and practice.

4) **Unquenchable Thirst** (v. 131). The psalmist "opened (his) mouth and panted" as he "longed for (God's) commandments." The world wears us down. Its ways can never truly satisfy. God's word alone satisfies the soul, bringing to an end an aimless and exhausting search for meaning.

5) **God's Mercy Revealed** (v. 132). Mercy can be defined as "not receiving the punishment we deserve." When we love the LORD and are not ashamed to wear His name, His mercy toward us abounds. Lovers of God are mercifully spared His ultimate judgment against the rebellious and wicked.

6) **Direction** (v. 133a). Remember how the psalmist panted and longed for God's commandments (v. 131)? Having one's steps directed by the LORD is the result. The psalmist was not interested in religious ritual or just an obligatory acknowledgement of the truth. He gave the LORD permission to direct his life.

7) **Victory Over Sin** (v. 133b). One tangible result of obeying God's direction is the

avoidance of and victory over sin in your life. Living by God's word enables us not to be dominated by temptation and sin. God's power through His word is more than enough to break those chains. Living by God's word does not make us immune to temptation, but it provides the ways and means not to be dominated by sin's destructive power.

8) **Redeemed from Man's Oppression** (v. 134). Here is God's hope for those who cannot avoid dealing with wicked people. Sinful people desire to see God's children stumble and fall. But the LORD provides deliverance from man's traps in order to freely worship and serve Him.

9) **Becoming a Friend of God** (v. 135). The psalmist's desire was to receive God's approval and favor. He wanted to cultivate a close relationship with the LORD. The best way to do that was to be taught more of God's statutes. Learn about God's ways and you will clearly see His character shine brightly through.

10) **Developing a Merciful Heart** (v. 136). The psalmist's heart was grieved as he observed people's rebellion against God and His law. His heart ached for God since His law was being rejected. His heart probably longed for people as he knew that the fruit

of sinful living would come upon them one day. Seeing people reject the only solution to life's emptiness and meaninglessness is hurtful. It's truly a time for tears.

Please, add your thoughts:

Day 18

Our Righteous Lord

Righteous are You, O LORD, and
upright are Your judgments.
Your testimonies, which You
have commanded, are righteous
and very faithful.
My zeal has consumed me, because my
enemies have forgotten Your words.
Your word is very pure; therefore
Your servant loves it.
I am small and despised, yet I
do not forget Your precepts.
Your righteousness is an everlasting
righteousness, and Your law is truth.
Trouble and anguish have overtaken me,
yet Your commandments are my delights.
The righteousness of Your
testimonies is everlasting; give me
understanding, and I shall live.

Psalm 119:137 - 144

Have you ever been accused (or accused someone else?) of being self-righteous? What does it mean to be righteous? According to the dictionary, righteous means to "act or be in accordance with what is just, honorable, and free from guilt or wrong." Does that describe you or someone you know?

The psalmist did not hesitate to not only declare the LORD Himself as righteous, but His judgments, too (v. 137). In other words, if the LORD is righteous then so is everything He does and says. The psalmist said, "Your testimonies...are righteous and very faithful" (v. 138). The LORD is righteous in every aspect of His being.

The psalmist's zeal for God's righteousness consumed him in two ways: 1) His enemies had forgotten God's words (v. 139) and 2) His love for the purity of God's word (v. 140). He was not ashamed to display his devotion to the LORD. Although he described himself as "small and despised" he never forgot the LORD's precepts (v. 141). He refused to compromise his convictions in the face of continuous opposition.

It is no coincidence that the psalmist tied together the LORD's "everlasting righteousness" and the truthfulness of His law (v. 142). His character is perfect. His words are perfect. His ways are perfect. And He never changes!

Following the Almighty Righteous LORD did not exempt the psalmist from "trouble and anguish," but he found his greatest delight in being comforted by His commandments (v. 143). Delight did not come from politics, entertainment, sports, worldly philosophy, drugs or any other form of escapism. It came from his relationship with the LORD.

Finally, the psalmist affirmed the everlasting righteousness of the LORD's testimonies. He made his decision to seek understanding and wisdom in order to live (v. 144).

How about you? Have you come to the place in your life of forsaking your own "righteousness?" Embrace God's everlasting righteousness and His unchanging truth for your life. What are you waiting for?

Please, add your thoughts:

Day 19

A Cry for Comfort

I cry out with my whole heart; hear me,
O LORD! I will keep Your statutes.
I cry out to You; save me, and I
will keep Your testimonies.
I rise before the dawning of the morning,
and cry for help; I hope in Your word.
My eyes awake through the night watches,
that I might meditate on Your word.
Hear my voice according to Your
lovingkindness; O LORD, revive
me according to Your justice.
They draw near who follow after
wickedness; they are far from Your law.
You are near, O LORD, and all Your
commandments are truth.
Concerning Your testimonies, I have known
of old that You have founded them forever.

Psalm 119:145 - 152

Do you pray? Why? To whom? How often? What kind of results do you expect to see?

The psalmist demonstrated a true reliance upon the LORD and expected Him to intervene in his life. He cried out with his "whole heart" (v. 145a) and held nothing back. He sought the LORD to save and help him (vv. 146, 147). The prayer life of the psalmist was not a dry routine or mindless and heartless ritual. He enjoyed communicating with the LORD, the Maker of heaven and earth and the only One qualified to provide help, guidance and protection in his time of need.

Prayer is an anytime and anywhere activity. It is not confined to a set time and place. The psalmist meditated on God's word "through the night watches" (v. 148) in order to gain a deeper insight or understanding of the LORD. This resulted in the psalmist confidently praying to God who demonstrated lovingkindness and justice (v. 149).

Why all of this crying out to the LORD for help, lovingkindness and justice? "They draw near who follow after wickedness; they are far from Your law" (v. 150). The psalmist has contended with his enemies throughout this psalm. His only source of comfort, strength and peace came from the LORD. He is nearer than the psalmist's (or our) enemies. His "commandments are truth" (v. 151) and His "testimonies have existed forever" (v. 152).

The psalmist chose to place His trust and confidence in the LORD and His truth rather than giving in to fear originating from wicked people. Prayer provided the hope for which his distressed heart longed. The LORD is near. His word is true and endures forever. Follow the example of many a person who plug into the only One who is willing and capable to provide "grace in our time of need" (Heb. 4:16).

Please, add your thoughts:

Day 20

Revival

Consider my affliction and deliver
me, for I do not forget Your law.
Plead my cause and redeem me;
revive me according to Your word.
Salvation is far from the wicked, for
they do not seek Your statutes.
Great are Your tender mercies, O LORD;
revive me according to Your judgments.
Many are my persecutors and my enemies,
yet I do not turn from Your testimonies.
I see the treacherous, and am disgusted,
because they do not keep Your word.
Consider how I love Your precepts;
revive me, O LORD, according
to Your lovingkindness.
The entirety of Your word is truth,
for every one of Your righteous
judgments endures forever.

Psalm 119:153 - 160

What methods do we use to overcome physical exhaustion? More sleep? Change of diet? More exercise? What about spiritual exhaustion? What methods do we use to overcome that?

The psalmist confidently approached the LORD with his burden. Even though he did not forget God's law he was still afflicted and burdened (v. 153). What was his plea? "Revive me according to Your word" (v. 154). When we read, study and apply the eternal word of God on a consistent basis, the burdens of life become more manageable. Why? Because we are ultimately entrusting ourselves to the most powerful Person who has endless resources to lift our burdens. Jesus said, "Come to Me, all you who labor and are heavy laden, and I will give you rest. Take My yoke upon you and learn from Me, for I am gentle and lowly in heart, and you will find rest for your souls. For My yoke is easy and My burden is light" (Matt. 11:28 - 30).

The wicked (those who are rebellious and disobedient toward the LORD) live life on their own terms and do not seek His statutes. Salvation (or deliverance) is far from them (v. 155). On the other hand, those people with the same strong faith in the LORD as the psalmist will be revived by His judgments and mercy (v. 156). Why? They cling to the LORD as their only hope, completely unashamed to be dependent upon Him to make it through life. Which camp do you belong to?

The psalmist provides us with a very important lesson in v. 157. We ought not to use the adversity in our lives as an excuse to turn away from the LORD. Trouble from his enemies drew him closer to the LORD and deeper into His word. We need to do likewise.

The psalmist observed the treacherous and was disgusted at their rebellion and disobedience toward the LORD and His word (v. 158). He did not use the fallacious reasoning that says, "You don't know their heart so you can't judge them." When speaking of false teachers Jesus said, "By their fruits you will know them" (Matt. 7:20). Be watchful but do not be bitter nor angry against those who are against you. When trouble in its many facets appears, believers should demonstrate a steadfast spirit marked by peace, joy and love. In short, we are called to follow in Jesus' footsteps.

Finally, the psalmist sought revival through the LORD's lovingkindness or mercy

(v. 159). "The LORD is merciful and gracious, slow to anger, and abounding in mercy" (Ps. 103:8). He shows unlimited goodness toward those whose hearts are committed to Him. That's why the psalmist rejoiced in the eternal truth of God's word (v. 160). He knew that only God's truth can bring about the genuine revival in mind and spirit that this world cannot. Hope is reborn as God's word revives the exhausted believer.

When hard times come into your life and hope is nowhere to be found, where do you search for revival?

Please, add your thoughts:

Day 21

Rejoice in God's Word

Princes persecute me without a cause,
but my heart stands in awe of Your word.
I rejoice at Your word as one
who finds great treasure.
I hate and abhor lying, but I love Your law.
Seven times a day I praise You, because
of Your righteous judgments.
Great peace have those who love Your law,
and nothing causes them to stumble.
LORD, I hope for Your salvation,
and I do Your commandments.
My soul keeps Your testimonies,
and I love them exceedingly.
I keep Your precepts and Your testimonies,
for all my ways are before You.

Psalm 119:161-168

What brings you the most joy in life? Marrying the love of your life? The birth of a child? Earning that long awaited promotion at the office? Watching your favorite football team scoring the winning points as time runs out?

By now it's no secret in whom and what caused the psalmist to rejoice. Despite the continuing persecution he suffered from those in power his heart stood in awe of God's word (v. 161). He even went so far as to rejoice over God's word as "one who finds great treasure" (v. 162). The psalmist hated lying but loved God's law, or truth (v. 163). He continually praised God for His "righteous judgments" (v. 164).

Why this outpouring of praise to God from the psalmist? From beginning to end he knew that God's word is absolute truth. Do we rejoice over God's eternal truth with the same zeal without regard for our circumstances and troubles?

Being in our self-consumed culture we are the ones who might ask the question: "What's in it for me if I obey God's law?" Two things:

1) "Great peace have those who love Your law" (v. 165a). You want real and lasting peace? Find it in God and His word.

2) "Nothing causes them to stumble" (v. 165b). Immerse yourself in God's word and you will stand firm throughout life's storms. If your roots grow deep in God's word you will bend but you will not break. Remember that "great peace" comes from a great God who is able to provide peace abundantly. His strength is more than sufficient to keep those who love and obey Him standing strong. "Nothing causes them to stumble."

Finally, loving God's word means practicing it. "I do Your commandments" (v. 166b). "My soul keeps Your testimonies" (vv. 167, 168a). Superficial sentimentality nor blind religious observance does not suffice. "All my ways are before You" (v. 168b). The LORD is the Maker of heaven and earth. He knows all of our thoughts, motives and intentions. Nothing is hidden from Him. Love for Him and His word will be shown by living it out.

Are we willing to practice what we preach?

Please, add your thoughts:

Day 22

In Conclusion...

Let my cry come before You, O LORD; give
me understanding according to Your word.
Let my supplication come before You;
deliver me according to Your word.
My lips shall utter praise, for You
teach me Your statutes.
My tongue shall speak of Your word, for
all Your commandments are righteous.
Let Your hand become my help, for
I have chosen Your precepts.
I long for Your salvation, O LORD,
and Your law is my delight.
Let my soul live, and it shall praise You;
and let Your judgments help me.
I have gone astray like a lost sheep;
seek Your servant, for I do not
forget Your commandments.

Psalm 119:169 - 176

Final words are important words. What final words would you say to your spouse, children, extended family and friends? Your final words would be carefully chosen in order for those you love to remember you affectionately and accurately. In closing out this song, the psalmist left his readers with four final words.

1) **Prayer**. The psalmist began this final section in a familiar way; he prayed. He cried out and brought his supplication to the LORD (vv. 169a, 170a). Unashamed to show his weakness and need, he asked the LORD to grant him both understanding and deliverance "according to Your word" (vv. 169b, 170b). He entrusted his whole being to the one and only LORD. Alternative methods were never considered.

2) **Praise**. Why did the psalmist praise the LORD so often? Through His word the psalmist learned the LORD's statutes and righteous commands (vv. 171, 172). The LORD's word provided the rock solid foundation the psalmist needed to overcome life's barriers, obstacles and persecutions. Fairy tales and fables don't have the power

to uphold and carry people during tough times. But God's eternal and unchanging truth does.

3) **Wait**. A major part of the Christian life requires waiting upon the LORD to provide help in His way and timing in our hour of need. The psalmist chose to wait on the hand of the LORD to be his help (v. 173). He knew that God didn't jump at his on-demand requests. The psalmist waited while delighting in God's law (v. 174). Waiting requires patience but yields the fruit of strength. "They that wait upon the LORD shall renew their strength; they shall mount up with wings as eagles; they shall run, and not be weary; and they shall walk, and not faint" (Isaiah 40:31).

4) **Mercy**. The psalmist sought the LORD's mercy in order to praise Him (v. 175). He admitted his waywardness but submitted his will to God, who sought those who had gone astray (v. 176). The LORD had demonstrated His mercy by providing His law. Following His ways was the only means the psalmist sought to experience a truly joyful and complete life.

What about us in today's world? The same rules apply. Only by complete surrender, dependence and obedience to God and His ways can we truly experience His mercy and love. The LORD is willing to extend His mercy to all people, but that offer is effective only in those who choose to receive it. This is

God's offer: Receive His mercy, grace and forgiveness in the Person of His Son, Jesus Christ. He is the fulfillment of Jewish messianic prophecy and manifestation of God's mercy. Allow His blood shed on the cross to cleanse you from your sins. Allow the reality of the Resurrection and the empty tomb to become your reality. When you allow Jesus complete and unhindered occupancy in your life you will experience life to the fullest both now and for eternity. What's your choice?

Please, add your thoughts:

Appendix A:
According to Your Word

The verse "According to Your word" occurs 12 times in Psalm 119. Take the time to memorize these verses as a reminder of how precious and powerful God's word is. And remember that the Author of these verses is an awesome God who loves you and desires you to get to know Him better. Memorization of His word can assist you with that.

1. "How can a young man cleanse his way? By taking heed according to Your word" (Ps. 119:9).

2. "My soul clings to the dust; revive me according to Your word" (Ps. 119:25).

3. "My soul melts from heaviness; strengthen me according to Your word" (Ps. 119:28).

4. "Let Your mercies come also to me, O LORD - Your salvation according to Your word" (Ps. 119:41).

5. "I entreated Your favor with my whole heart; be merciful to me according to Your word" (Ps. 119:58).

6. "You have dealt well with Your servant, O LORD, according to Your word" (Ps. 119:65).

7. "Let, I pray, Your merciful kindness be my comfort, according to Your word to Your servant" (Ps. 119:76).

8. "I am afflicted very much; revive me, O LORD, according to Your word" (Ps. 119:107).

9. "Uphold me according to Your word, that I may live; and do not let me be ashamed of my hope" (Ps. 119:116).

10. "Plead my cause and redeem me; revive me according to Your word" (Ps. 119:154).

11. "Let my cry come before You, O LORD; give me understanding according to Your word" (Ps. 119:169).

12. Let my supplication come before You; deliver me according to Your word" (Ps. 119:170).